The Illegitimate Players present

OF GRAPES AND NUTS

*Doug Armstrong
Keith Cooper
& Tom Willmorth*

BROADWAY PLAY PUBLISHING INC
224 E 62nd St, NY, NY 10065
www.broadwayplaypub.com
info@broadwayplaypub.com

OF GRAPES AND NUTS
© 1991, 2000 by The Illegitimate Players

All rights reserved. This work is fully protected under the copyright laws of the United States of America. No part of this publication may be photocopied, reproduced, stored in a retrieval system, or transmitted, in any form or by any means, electronic, mechanical, recording, or otherwise, without the prior permission of the publisher. Additional copies of this play are available from the publisher.

Written permission is required for live performance of any sort. This includes readings, cuttings, scenes, and excerpts. For amateur and stock performances, please contact Broadway Play Publishing Inc. For all other rights contact...

Book design: Marie Donovan
Page make-up: Adobe Indesign
Typeface: Palatino
Copy editing: Michele Travis

OF GRAPES AND NUTS was first presented by The Illegitimate Players (producers Maureen FitzPatrick and Kathy Giblin) on 3 November 1990 at the Victory Gardens Studio Theater in Chicago, Illinois. The cast and creative contributors were:

CAT DRIVER	Maureen FitzPatrick
TOM JOAD	Tom Willmorth
LENNY	Keith Cooper
JIM CASY	Doug Armstrong
MA JOAD	Maureen Morley
PA JOAD	Doug Armstrong
COMPANY MAN	Paul Stroili
MAE	Maureen FitzPatrick
GUS	Paul Stroili
AL	Tom Willmorth
BORDER GUARD	Paul Stroili
CURLY	Maureen FitzPatrick
CANDY	Paul Stroili
Director	Paul Frellick
Set design	Doug Armstrong
Lighting design	Jennifer E Tanzer
Costume design & stage management	Kathy Giblin
Sound design	Jeff Tamraz
Original music	Bill Haas

SYNOPSIS OF SCENES

ACT ONE

Scene One: The Joad place, Salisaw, Oklahoma
Scene Two: A roadside diner, three weeks later
Scene Three: A California border station, several days later

ACT TWO

A bunkhouse on a California fruit ranch

AUTHORS' NOTE

The characters, locations, and story line depicted in this play are not intended to represent persons either living or dead, or the works of certain famous American authors, either living or dead, especially those who are dead but are survived by a spouse who may be short on a sense of humor but long on legal representation.

A NOTE ON THE CHARACTERS

The characters in this play are based on original characters created by John Steinbeck in *The Grapes of Wrath* and *Of Mice and Men*. For the most part, they closely reflect their source characters, but a few are composites of two or more of Steinbeck's originals. The play was written so that it may be performed by a cast of six actors, with four playing multiple roles.

CAT DRIVER is loosely based on the truck driver TOM JOAD hitches a ride from in *The Grapes of Wrath*. In this case, however, the driver is played by a woman.

TOM JOAD is essentially the same character as in *The Grapes of Wrath*, although here he also assumes the role of friend and caretaker to LENNY that the character George played in *Of Mice and Men*.

LENNY is based on the character Lennie from *Of Mice and Men*. He is large in stature but small of mind, unusually fond of rabbits and highly protective of his friend TOM JOAD.

JIM CASY is based on the character from *The Grapes of Wrath*. He is a born preacher who has found a new religion in the labor movement.

MA JOAD is based on the character from *The Grapes of Wrath*. She is the unwavering spirit that holds the Joad clan together.

PA JOAD is based more on the character of Grampa than that of Pa Joad in *The Grapes of Wrath*. He is a stubborn and somewhat senile old man, prone to knee-slapping.

COMPANY MAN is generally based on figures of authority, such as sheriff's deputies, in *The Grapes of Wrath*. Here, though, he more closely resembles a modern corporate flunky.

MAE is based on the character of the same name in *The Grapes of Wrath*. She is a veteran diner waitress, easily irritated but kind-hearted, with a special affection for truck drivers.

GUS is based on the truck driver Big Bill the Rat from *The Grapes of Wrath*. He is gregarious and outspoken.

AL is based on Al the diner cook from *The Grapes of Wrath*. He is gruff and crotchety, and probably smokes while cooking.

BORDER GUARD is based on similar guards found in *The Grapes of Wrath*. He is a no-nonsense, by-the-book type of officer.

CURLY is based largely on the character Curley from *Of Mice and Men*. However, since the character here is a woman, she also takes on some of the traits of Curley's wife from the same play. She is an ill-tempered and dominating task-mistress, who reveals a softer side only to LENNY.

CANDY is a composite of the ranch hands from *Of Mice and Men*, such as Candy and Slim. He is polite and somewhat reserved.

A NOTE ON THE PLAY

This play, like any other, is open to a wide range of interpretation. However, it has been our experience that the script works best when played straight. As Peter Ustinov so succinctly put it, "Comedy is simply a funny way of being serious."

ACT ONE

Scene One

(Setting: A tiny, dilapidated farm house seemingly in the middle of nowhere. It is empty. In the dark we hear the rumbling engine of a bulldozer coming to a halt. The lights come up to reveal TOM *and the* CAT DRIVER *standing before the house. The* CAT DRIVER *wears dusty coveralls, a hardhat and goggles.)*

CAT DRIVER: It ain't the heat...it's the humility.

TOM: Still, this is where we git out. 'Preciate the ride and all.

CAT DRIVER: Well, I saw you boys hitchin' at the truck stop, I couldn't just drive off.

TOM: Well, we thank ya. Ain't never traveled in no bulldozer before.

CAT DRIVER: It's a Cat.

TOM: A Cat?

CAT DRIVER: The Cat 500 Autolux earth mover. Slower'n a bitch, but fun to maneuver. *(Looking about)* Sure this is where you're goin', pal? This crappy ol' deserted squatter house?

TOM: Lived here all my life.

CAT DRIVER: Nice place. Big ol' parking lot over there for the kids to play on.

TOM: That ain't no parkin' lot, that's my Pa's farmland. Dust done choked it, that's all. Once it's hosed off it'll be fine. Ma! Pa! ...Where is ever'body? What's with these here crates in the yard? Pa!

CAT DRIVER: *(Looking toward Cat)* Hey, you idiot!

TOM: You see Pa?

CAT DRIVER: Nah, it's your friend messin' with my rig.

TOM: Git over here Lenny! That ain't no toy. Come here!

CAT DRIVER: Must be tough travelin' across the state with him.

TOM: Naw, Lenny's a right guy. Kinda like him along.

CAT DRIVER: I mean him havin' to sit on your lap the whole ride. Sorry about the lack of room.

*(*LENNY *runs on stage.)*

TOM: Lenny?

LENNY: Wha..?

TOM: What you got behind your back?

LENNY: Nuttin'.

TOM: You still got that dead mouse, don't you? I done throw'd it away once. Give it here.

*(*LENNY *slowly hands over a lever from the Cat.)*

CAT DRIVER: Hey, that's my brake lever!

TOM: Lenny, you go put that back where you found it.

LENNY: Okay, Joad. Sorry, Mister. *(He exits.)*

CAT DRIVER: Hey...

TOM: Don't pay him no mind. He's jus' a might slow, tha's all. *(Peering into house)* What the hell? The house been cleared out.

ACT ONE 3

CAT DRIVER: Your folks probably up and went West where the farming's good. All the land 'round here is dry as my granny's ovums.

TOM: My folks wouldn'ta gone. Don't matter how tough it gits to farm, we know we belongs to the land, and the land we belongs to is grand. We put more than seed into this dirt. We put in toil and sweat. Blood, too, and the bones of our kin who died workin' it. What more can folks put into their land?

CAT DRIVER: Ever think of tryin' phosphates?

TOM: Still, they wouldn't a moved. Our soul's in this place. Even though I've been gone fer five years, without a word from my family, my soul's still here.

CAT DRIVER: That's right touching. *(Beat)* Look, if your buddy is gettin' out here too, I gotta get goin'.

TOM: Yeah, I betcha yer achin' to know where I was fer five years. Aren't ya?!

CAT DRIVER: No, not really. *(To* LENNY*)* Hey Bonehead! I thought I tol' ya to get out of there.

TOM: Oh, sure yer curious to know. I seen it in yer face ever since you picked us up. Yer bladder's ready to bust needin' to know where I been fer five years. Five years gone. How's he gonna explain that, yer sayin' to yerself. New set o' clothes, state issued. Yer jus' scratchin' yer fuzzy neck thinkin'—what's the guy's secret? What's behind his eyes?

CAT DRIVER: *(To* TOM*)* Look, Pal, could you tell—

TOM: Prison! That's right, prison.

CAT DRIVER: Pardon?

TOM: Naw. Paroled.

LENNY: *(Entering excitedly)* I seen a rabbit hutch! I seen a rabbit hutch! I seen a rabbit hutch!

TOM: Calm down, Lenny.

LENNY: Can I go pet the rabbits, Joad?

TOM: Hold on, Lenny. First off we ought to pay the lady fer the ride.

CAT DRIVER: Oh, there's no need. Happy to do it.

LENNY: Is she a lady? I thought she were a man. She looks jus' like a man I know'd once.

TOM: Lenny.

LENNY: What was his name?

TOM: I 'pologize fer Lenny, he's a little—

CAT DRIVER: It's no bother.

LENNY: Butch! That's it! You look like Butch!

CAT DRIVER: Make it ten bucks for gas money.

TOM: *(Sighs and takes out some bills)* Damn it, Lenny.

LENNY: Sorry, Lady. It's just 'cause yer hair was hid under yer hat, so I goofed.

CAT DRIVER: *(Takes off hardhat, shaking down her hair)* Well now ya know.

(LENNY *is instantly engrossed by the* CAT DRIVER's *hair. He moves slowly behind her, studying, then touching her head.)*

TOM: *(Gives* CAT DRIVER *money)* Don't pay Lenny no heed. He's simple. Ain't got much in the way of a mind, but what's on it he speaks, and I'm respectful of that. Done time in McAlester together, looked after each other I guess. Yeah, I betcher wonderin' what it was I done got me locked up. Sure you are. Yer just hemorrhagin' to hear tell o' my crime.

CAT DRIVER: It really don't matter.

TOM: Homo-cide.

ACT ONE

(LENNY's *hand becomes entangled in* CAT DRIVER's *hair. He tries to yank it free.*)

CAT DRIVER: *(Inhales rapidly)* Ahhhhh!

TOM: But it were self defense.

CAT DRIVER: *(Pointing at hair)* Wahhhhh!

TOM: *(Noticing* LENNY*)* Lenny!

CAT DRIVER: Wahh!

LENNY: Tom!

CAT DRIVER: Wahh!

LENNY: Tom!

TOM: Lenny! Let go of her hair!

(LENNY *lets go of* CAT DRIVER's *hair. She falls to the ground.*)

LENNY: I'm sorry, I'm sorry. I didn't mean to, Joad. I was just petting her hair and I was being careful like you told me and nothing came off in my hand and, and...

TOM: Calm down, Lenny!

LENNY: ...It weren't like what happened in Weed. Honest.

TOM: Quiet Lenny! Look, why don't you go see if there are any rabbits in that ol' hutch 'round back.

LENNY: Okay, Joad! Oh boy...oh boy oh boy.

(LENNY *runs off stage happily.*)

CAT DRIVER: Excuse me. Did he say—

TOM: Nothin' happened in Weed!

CAT DRIVER: No. Did he say your name's Joad?

TOM: I'm young Tom Joad, Old Tom's boy.

CAT DRIVER: In that case, could you please sign right here?

(CAT DRIVER *takes a form out of her pocket and hands it to* TOM, *who signs it.*)

TOM: Lenny gits a little excitable when he sees a lady's hair. He's workin' on it.

CAT DRIVER: Sure.

TOM: *(Signing)* Sometimes he don't know his own strength.

CAT DRIVER: Not good. *(Takes form from* TOM*)*

(CAT DRIVER *approaches the house, pulls off the last page of the form, which clearly reads* CONDEMNED BY OWNER *and slaps it onto the house.*)

TOM: Hey, what's that go to say? Who's makin' decisions 'bout what we can build on our own land?!

CAT DRIVER: It's not your land any more. The mortgage on this tract got foreclosed by the Squawnee Land and Cattle Company which has contracted me to remove all structures. You've been kicked off.

TOM: By a company? That ain't right.

CAT DRIVER: *(Checks the second sheet of the form for a moment)* Yeah it is. Guess that explains them moving crates.

TOM: This is Joad land! Three generations of Joadses were born here. We carved out the drinkin' well with our fingers, sixty feet deep. Pa's teeth are made outta gravel found on this land. Ma raised chickens here, and goats and pigs. One time a pig got loose and run into the house and ate a baby. Disgustin' things like that is what makes family history, and family history is what makes ownership. We owns this place.

CAT DRIVER: I'm sorry, Mr Joad, but we got regulations.

TOM: Git off this land now or God help me I'm gonna—

ACT ONE 7

CAT DRIVER: What, break yer parole and commit homo-side again? You can't even pronounce it let alone do it.

TOM: *(Calling off)* Hey, Lenny! Come here and see how soft and luxurious Butch's hair is.

CAT DRIVER: We'll be back, Joad.

TOM: I count on it.

(CAT DRIVER *runs off. Bulldozer engine sounds erupt and fade.)*

LENNY: *(Entering)* Weren't no rabbits, but I found a pig... She leaving, Joad? Did I hurt her feelings?

TOM: Naw.

LENNY: Her spine?

TOM: Naw, she just left is all. Probably gonna stop at all the neighbors farms and kick them off too.

LENNY: I ain't so sure she'll be stoppin', Joad.

TOM: Why's that?

(LENNY *pulls brake lever out from behind his back.)*

TOM: Lenny!... What else you got in yer pocket?

LENNY: Nuttin'.

TOM: Show me.

LENNY: Jus' this mouse.

TOM: Give it here. *(He throws mouse off stage.)* The trouble with mice is ya always kill 'em. What else you got in there? You smell like a small rodeo.

LENNY: *(Reluctantly)* A baby chick, a goldfish, another baby chick, a road turtle...oh, and a matchbook that Lady gave me in Weed.

TOM: *(Grabs matchbook)* Give me that. You ain't supposed to play with them.

LENNY: Matches?

TOM: No. Ladies! I seen what you did to that driver. Remember what I told you about women?

LENNY: That I ain't s'posed to touch 'em too hard, they ain't like rabbits, and if I forget the first rule and something bad happens, I hav'ta go hide.

TOM: Hide where?

LENNY: Uh... Don't tell me...in the cave in the river bed!

TOM: That's right.

LENNY: The one you showed me. The one I hided in after I done bad in Weed.

TOM: But that's a secret and we ain't goin' to bring it up in front of nobody.

LENNY: Right, Joad. *(Pause)* Joad?

TOM: Yeah?

LENNY: What happened in Weed that I done bad?

TOM: You can't recall that?

LENNY: I 'member we got outta prison and we walked into that bar in Weed. And I asked you if I could pet the rabbits and you said "Sure." Then some cops came and we had to hide. But what did I do that was bad? I just petted the rabbit.

TOM: Well, dammit Lenny, how was I to know Weed Oklahoma had a Playboy club.

(CASY's *voice is heard singing offstage.*)

CASY: Yes Sir, that's my Savior
Be on yer best behavior
Yes Sir, that's my Savior now.

LENNY: Listen. Somebody's singin'. Is it yer Pa?

TOM: No, Pa ain't no crooner.

(LENNY *and* TOM *hide.* CASY *enters, carrying a knapsack.*)

# ACT ONE

CASY: Sa-tan, git thee behind me
Jez-bell, rope and bind me
Let's go where they can't find me now
(He breaks into dance step.)
Jes-us, yer crown was thorny
Popped up on Easter morny
Since I quit preachin', I never git horny now.

(LENNY *and* TOM *show themselves.*)

TOM: What are you doin here?

CASY: *(Alarmed)* Don't shoot! Ain't doin' nothin'. I'm here to...check the meter, I'm with the gas company.... No, the cattle company, I'm here to check the cattle....I mean take soil samples. *(Scoops up a little dirt)* There, got some! Best git back to the lab now. Jus' don't shoot.

TOM: What're you blatherin' 'bout. We ain't shootin' nobody.

CASY: You ain't cops?

TOM: Nah, we ain't cops.

CASY: Is ya on the lam?

LENNY: I ain't been on a lamb since that time at the petting zoo.

TOM: Lenny! ...We ain't wanted, an' we ain't lookin' fer no trouble. You live around here?

CASY: Here abouts.

TOM: You wouldn't happen to know how long this place been empty, would ya?

CASY: Most people 'round here got run off weeks ago. Didn't want to stop along the road myself, 'fraid the cops or land company guys'd arrest me fer trespass. Say, ain't this the Joad place?

TOM: Tha's right.

LENNY: Maybe he knows where your Ma and Pa went, Joad.

CASY: Joad? Well, grease my palm with a slab o' bacon, it's young Tom Joad! You been in prison as I recollect it.

TOM: Jus' got out a few weeks ago.

CASY: Ya bust out?!

TOM: No, paroled.

CASY: *(Disappointed)* Oh. Still, you's out. And you shouldn't-a-been there in the first place, anyhow. You only whacked that guy with a shovel 'cause he knifed ya first.

TOM: *(Angry)* Hey, how come you know so much about me anyway?

CASY: You wouldn't remember me I guess. The Sunday I give you the Holy Spirit I picked a real long scripture verse and held you underwater 'til I spoked it all. You was in a coma fer a day or two, but you come out saved.

TOM: Why you're the preacher.

CASY: I was a preacher, but I ain't no more. Reverend Jim Casy—was once your average tongue speakin', bush burnin', tent packin', bread breakin', grape juice pourin' crackpot fer Jesus. Used to baptize two hundred souls at a time in the irrigation canal screamin' my guts out. You prob'ly remember that.

TOM: No.

CASY: You gotta remember the time I preached from the hay loft, walkin' on my hands, with a wasp nest stuck over my head?

TOM: Maybe heard it mentioned.

ACT ONE

CASY: You hav'ta recollect the Sunday I baptized forty souls a minute at the fair ground's water slide, did benediction from the top of a power pole, then lit myself on fire and dove ninety feet into a bucket of icy communion.

TOM: Oh, okay! "Revelation Jim—The Daredevil Disciple."

CASY: Not no more. I lost the call o' the Sperit. *(Pulls out a flask)* Abused it so's I lost it. Mind if I squat?

(CASY and TOM squat down. CASY drinks from the flask and hands it to TOM.)

CASY: I used to lead them tent meetin's, never took a collection or nothin', just workin' everybody into a big lather. But damn if ever' time I went to lay down outside the tent, some gal'd come and lay down with me. Their souls was all hopped up with the glory of the meetin' one minute, the next minute we're out back in the grass doin' the Gomorrah. And I starts to think, wait up, Preacher. These people trusts you and needs guidance. You can't take advantage of their frenzy fer a quick one. But jus' soon's I think that, Li'l Jesu of the Trouser had resurrected his self and I'm back there shtupin' the Ladies League.

TOM: Sounds like you been bearin' more'n a cross.

CASY: I was bearin' doubts, Tom. I got to thinkin' that maybe there ain't no sin or virtue. Maybe they's just things folks do. And maybe what I should be servin' ain't the Holy Sperit, but the human sperit. 'Cause maybe folks don't have a soul of their own, but we's all part of a big soul.

TOM: Yeah, and maybe you're gonna burn in hell, Casy.

CASY: Well, all I knows is that I got to serve the people. How 'bout you Tom? What you figger to do now you're out of prison?

LENNY: Oh, we gonna raise rabbits! Joad, tell 'im what it's gonna be like when we git to yer folks farm.

TOM: We are at my folks farm, Lenny.

LENNY: *(Looks around curiously, then laughs)* Good one, Joad! Tell 'im about our farm, okay? Tell 'im 'bout the rabbits.

TOM: Aw, Lenny, you knows it by heart, you tell it.

LENNY: Okay. Okay. Okay. *(Pause)* Okay.

TOM: One day we'll...

LENNY: One day we'll git a place, finest forty acres you ever seen. Don't have to git up if we don't want and if we want to we can. There will be corn, and hay, and—I'm skippin' ahead, Joad, to the rabbit part—and we'll have rabbits, millions of 'em. Red 'n yellow, black 'n white, and we'll grow alfalfa and I'll pick it and feed it to the rabbits. And we'll eat what we grow and we'll live off the fatta the land. The end.

CASY: Sounds like a nice farm. And if the land goes dry you can turn it into a camp fer special children.

LENNY: Can I go play with the pig now, Joad?

TOM: I guess. But be careful, ya can't handle a pig like a would an accordion. They don't take to it.

LENNY: Ho, boy. Bye, Preacher.

CASY: I ain't no damn preacher!

(LENNY exits.)

TOM: Casy, yer welcome to stay on and join us here at the farm. Once I find Ma and Pa we're goin' to turn this place into somethin' real good.

ACT ONE 13

CASY: I'd love to Tom, but I got me a new callin'. I lef' my congregation so's I could serve the common man. Folks whose only religion is their own two hands, who don't have a home no more, or a job, or a paternity suit 'ginst me. I'm gonna serve the people by bein' out there amongst the people.

TOM: *(Peering into the distance)* Speakin' of people, we got one comin' up the road.

CASY: Tom, we gotta hide. If we run out into the field and lay flat they won't see us.

TOM: I ain't hidin'. This is my own house and it's my right to be—

CASY: They don't give a cuss about rights, Tom! They got guns and they'll use 'em too. Got guns and tear gas and bulldozers! We can't fight 'em.

TOM: Looks like an ol' woman in a sundress.

CASY: It's a disguise, Tom. Prob'ly a cop in drag comin' to drive us off.

TOM: This hidin' out's got you paranoid, Casy.

CASY: Look, if'n you're fixin' to fight 'em, best of luck. But, I gotta be followin' my new callin', which I think is this way. *(He indicates the opposite direction from the approaching stranger.)* Good bye, Tom.

TOM: You too, Prea— *(He gets a nasty look from* CASY.*)* Guy-who-was-until-recently-a-preacher.

(CASY *exits.*)

TOM: Well, I'll be damned... Ma!

(MA *enters.*)

MA: *(Seeing* TOM*)* Praise God fer victory! Tommy's come home! *(She rubs* TOM*'s cheeks)* Is you wanted, Tommy? Did ya bust out?

TOM: No, Ma, paroled.

MA: *(Disappointed)* Oh.

TOM: *(Looking back up the road)* Ma, where was you at? Where's Pa, and Granma?

MA: Well, we all went to town to buy a truck. We're fixin' to head west, Tommy, to California. We was gonna write to tell you. Even had the letter all writ and sealed up and made out to Tom Joad, Murderer, care of McAlester State Prison. But times been hard lately, and after we paid fer the truck, we didn't have the money fer a stamp. Thank God we didn't leave without ya.

TOM: Where's Pa then?

MA: He'n Granma's drivin' back. I wanted to git here 'fore the sun went down so I walked. It ain't a very good truck, Tom. But it'll do to git us to California.

TOM: Why California?

MA: *(She pulls out a flyer.)* It were this han'bill we got. Says they need plenty of men to pick peaches in California. Pay good wages too. Sounds a might bit better than what we got, Tommy.

TOM: But this is our land here. Seems like we're backin' down from a fair fight, Ma.

MA: There's nothin' left fer us here, Tommy. The land's dead and all your brothers and sisters moved off. Noah went to Oklahoma City three years ago fer 'frigerator repair school, but we never heard back. Al joined the army to see the world. Got stationed in Tulsa. And your sister, Rose of Magnesia, she run off with some dairyman from upstate, and that's the last time in my life I will mention her name. The fambly's bustin' up, Tommy. You's the only one left.

TOM: Well, I'm here fer good, Ma.

MA: Tommy, I got to ask you—you ain't mad?

TOM: Mad, Ma?

ACT ONE 15

MA: You ain't poisoned mad? You don't hate nobody? They didn' do nothin' in that there prison to rot you out with crazy mad?

TOM: *(Pauses)* Naw, I weren't proud like some fellas. I let stuff run off'n me. Why, what's the matter, Ma?

MA: I knowed Purty Boy Floyd. I knowed his ma. They was good folks. Sure, he was full of hell, like any good boy, that is until folks got after 'im. He done a little bad thing once an' they hurt him, caught 'im an' hurt him so's he was mad, an' the next time he done somethin' bad they hurt him again, an' when that made him madder they up and hurt him some more. Before you knowed it, he was mean-mad. He weren't no boy nor man no more, just a walkin' chunk of mean-mad, a snarlin' an' a snappin' worse than them folks at the post office. Still, they wouldn't let up on him. They kept a shootin' an' a spittin' an' a flickin' things at him 'til he was nothin' but a hot chunk of mean-mad, just roastin' an' boilin' in his own juices o' hate, sizzlin' like side-meat in a red-hot fry pan of scorn—

TOM: *(Interrupting her)* Ma! ...How long's it been since you ate?

MA: I just got to know, Tommy. Did they hurt you like that? Did they turn you into a crazy chunk of mean-mad?

TOM: No Ma, I ain't like that. All the time in prison I pretty much kept to myself. Didn't cuss nobody, didn't cross nobody. Guess you could say I was what they call a pansy, but it kept me out of trouble.

MA: Thank God.

TOM: *(Grabs shovel)* Still, when I seen what they was doin' to the house, I near wanted to—

MA: *(Takes shovel away)* Tommy, don't you go an' try to fight 'em on your own. They's no use in it. We been stayin' over at your Uncle John's place near a month now. We just come back to pack up the truck.

(Sound of pig squealing is heard offstage.)

TOM: Lenny, git on over here an' leave that pig be!

MA: Who'n you talkin' to, Tom?

TOM: That there's Lenny; jus' a guy I met in Prison. Simple-minded fella, but works hard and speaks his mind.

(LENNY enters.)

TOM: Lenny, wasn't you listenin' when I told you 'bout treatin' pigs like an accordion?

LENNY: I sure was, Joad, but you didn't say nothin' about a harmonica.

TOM: Lenny, this here's my ma. Ma, this is Lenny.

MA: How do you do, Lenny?

(LENNY approaches MA—she raises shovel as a shield.)

MA: Any friend of Tommy's is welcome here.

(TOM takes shovel from MA and leans it against house.)

LENNY: Thanks, this is a real purty place you got here, I mean, had here, Mrs Ma...er, Mrs Joad Ma....

MA: Ma is fine.

LENNY: Glad to hear it, so is Lenny.

TOM: Look, Ma, somethin' drivin' up the road.

LENNY: Maybe it's the Wells Fargo Wagon with something special just fer me!

MA: No it's Pa fer sure. I can smell the clutch burning.

(Engine sounds offstage of old truck pulling up and sputtering to a stop.)

PA: *(Offstage)* Gol dang it!!

MA: *(Calling off to PA)* Say, Pa, look who we got here!

ACT ONE 17

PA: *(Offstage)* Well, would you look at that!

TOM: *(Calling off)* Hi, Pa.

PA: *(Entering)* Would you look at that! Who's the gol dang fool done left them big hickeys on the side o' my best sow!

(MA *glares at* LENNY, *who tries to look nonchalant.*)

MA: Look Pa, Tommy done come home from prison!

PA: *(Looking at* LENNY*)* Tommy? Why, you've changed, boy! Prison done changed you, didn't it Tommy? You're different somehow...

MA: Pa, can't you even...

PA: I know, it's the haircut! Dang two-bit prison hair cut can make any man look a fool. *(He gives* LENNY's *cheeks a rub.)* Oh, we missed you somethin' fierce, Tommy.

TOM: Git a holt a yerself, Pa. I'm over here.

PA: *(Turns and crosses to* TOM*)* Tommy. It is you! Say, did'ja bust out?

TOM: No. But I'm startin' to wish to God I had, though.

PA: Tommy, I need to know somethin'. *(Whispers to* TOM*)* Who's the big guy back there I just gave the Happy Rub to?

TOM: That there's Lenny, friend of mine from prison.

PA: Lordy.

TOM: Came out with me to work the place, now Ma says we's leavin'. Why didn't ya stand your ground?

PA: Hell, I did! Pissed in the gas tank of ever' CAT they drove on the place. Trouble was, I'd been drinkin' yer Uncle John's corn whiskey, so's all it done was improve their fuel efficiency by forty percent.

MA: Ever'body shut yer yaps! We got us a Buick a drivin' up the road.

PA: Company man! Where's my gun, where's my gun?! *(Exits into house)*

TOM: Ma, you and Lenny go inside. I'll handle this.

(Sound offstage of car pulling up and car door slamming.)

MA: I'm stayin' with you, Tommy. We's all in this fix together.

LENNY: I'm not. *(Exits into house)*

(COMPANY MAN enters, carrying a briefcase and sheet of paper.)

MA: What can we do fer you, mister?

COMPANY MAN: Well, for starters, you can get the hell off this property before sundown.

TOM: Says who?

COMPANY MAN: *(Handing* TOM *paper)* Says this here order from the land owners. The Cat driver we sent out earlier came back yelling that you're trying to resist.

TOM: She said that, did she?

COMPANY MAN: Close as we can tell. She was screaming something about you before she buzzed right past us and hit the gasoline dump.

MA: Wait just a minute here...ain't you Joe Keating's boy?

COMPANY MAN: So what if I am?

MA: What the hell you out running your own people off the land for?

COMPANY MAN: Times is hard, ma'am. A man's got to do what he can to provide for his own family. I got me a wife an' two kids, and they've got to eat the same as yours, and with both of them in private boarding

ACT ONE 19

school...it's tough. Got to make payments on three cars and a motor boat, and that ain't even to mention the summer home or the house in the Poconos...

PA: *(Entering from house with a gun)* I'll give you Poconose! Poke yer nose full-a lead, ya good-fer-nothin'! Oughta kill you here fer trespass!

COMPANY MAN: Wouldn't do no good, mister. Even if you killed me, they're graduating four more like me every day to take my place.

MA: Maybe we could talk to your boss, talk to the person owns this land.

COMPANY MAN: Ain't just one person owns it. It's the Squawnee Land & Cattle Company owns it.

MA: Well, who owns that there cattle company you speak of?

COMPANY MAN: Ain't just one person owns that, neither. Cattle company owners go by the name of Lincoln Savings & Loan.

PA: Then I'll kill the boss of that there savin's & loan!

COMPANY MAN: Ain't got just one boss there neither.

PA: Well somebody gots to be in charge at a savin's and loan!

COMPANY MAN: Not necessarily. They got what they call a "Board a Directors." There's an outside chance you can talk with one of them, that is, if your willing to go back east and hire a lobbyist.

PA: Gol dang it!

MA: Well, who can my husband kill?!

TOM: It don't seem right... Somehow it don't seem right to my way of thinkin' that a man can work hard all his life, carvin' a homestead out of forty acres of burnt-out soil, only to git pushed off by some so-called "Board of

Dissectors." It don't seem right 'cause it ain't just our land we're losin', it's our soul; an' when a man's got no soul he ain't good fer nothin' but middle management. Hell of a way to do business.

COMPANY MAN: Tell that to our stockholders, Goober. It's not for me to decide. Can't erase the bottom line.

PA: I'll erase your bottom line if'n you don't git off this land right now, you double-breasted varmint!

COMPANY MAN: Old man, this is you're final notice—

PA: I'll give you final notice, you....

COMPANY MAN: If I have to come back again I'm bringing the sheriff with a warrant for your arrests. Good day. *(He exits.)*

PA: I'll good day you, you...durn good day...stupid dummy!

MA: We's even hard up fer comebacks, Tommy. *(To PA)* Pa, put that gun away and load up the truck. It's time we was leavin'.

TOM: Looks like we ain't got no choice, Pa.

PA: If'n we gotta go, then we gotta go. I jus' don't like bein' pushed off.

MA: It's fer the best, Tommy. *(Takes out handbill)* Maybe California's jus' what this fambly needs.

PA: *(Grabbing handbill)* Your ma's right. See here, Tommy? Good pay, lots a' work, advancement opportunity, career placement. Eighty degrees all year long so's we don't git rhummy-tism. Ma's set on gettin' herself one a them little white houses with orange trees all around it. As fer me, soon's we git there, I'm gonna grab me a bunch of grapes and jus' a smear 'em all over my face. Jus' squish 'em all over my face till they gits all pulpy and I git seeds in my eyes and they start a stingin' and turnin' red and stains my face purple!

ACT ONE 21

Then I'll git me some melons and bust 'em over my head—don't know why, but I will!

MA: If'n we squeeze real hard we can all fit in the truck, and the four of us'll be a fambly again.

TOM: Four? Granma ain't comin'?

MA: Four. You, me, Pa and Granma. Who else we countin'? Oh, not the behemoth, Tommy.

TOM: Lenny'n me been travelin' together. I kinda promised him work when we got here to the farm.

PA: Hell, he can have the damn place!

TOM: Lenny's a good worker, Pa. Strong, too. Be a hell of a farm hand if'n we find jobs that don't require power tools. *(Calling off)* Lenny, come out here!

PA: Tommy, there just ain't no room.

LENNY: *(Entering from house)* Yeah, Joad?

TOM: Lenny, we's discussin' our travelin' plans...

LENNY: Oh yeah, Joad and me are gonna find ourselves a little place to settle down, finest forty acres you ever seen. *(To* TOM*)* Just you an' me and a hutch full o' rabbits, right, Joad?

MA: Tommy, you sure prison didn't change you none?

TOM: Lenny, we can't raise no rabbits here, so we's goin' to California. Thing is, Pa don't think you should come along.

LENNY: *(To* PA*)* You what?

TOM: And the decision's Pa's to make.

LENNY: *(Appealing to* PA*)* Why can't I come Mr Pa? Joad says I'm a good worker, and back in prison he taught me to control myself real good, and not crush nobody's skull with my bare hands just because I didn't git my way.

PA: Well, it ain't set in stone, or nothin'. *(To* TOM*)* Tommy, can I have a word with ya?

(PA *and* TOM *step aside.)*

PA: It's jus' tha' I'm worried, son. Don't think the family should be travelin' with no jail bird ex-con... who ain't related.

TOM: Lenny ain't no con.

PA: Then why was he in prison?

TOM: *(Out loud)* Weren't his fault. Lenny was livin' outside o' McAlester, workin' fer a laundry delivery service. One time he's droppin' off linen at the Big House, and Lenny bein' slow and all, his Aunt Clara'd stenciled his phone number on his jacket so's he won't forget it. Hell, warden sees a guy walkin' 'round the yard with a number on his chest, he ain't gettin' out. So I looked after him, and took to him, I guess. Promised him a job with us. Maybe I spoke out of turn, Pa, but I gave him my word as a Joad.

PA: Well there's our out right there!

MA: Now, Pa, let the boy come along. They mus' be a box o' stuff here worth sacrificing so's Lenny can fit a'board. We can make do without a belongin', but not without a kindness.

LENNY: Can I take the pig with us to California, Joad?

PA: Don't push it, boy! We got enough salt pork loaded already. That there pig we'll jus' hav'ta destroy 'fore we leave. I best see to it now.

(PA *checks to see that gun is loaded, and exits.* LENNY *turns to* TOM *aghast.)*

TOM: Now Lenny, sometimes it's better to kill somethin' than to leave it to suffer on it's own. I'm sure it'd be happier if'n we shot it.

LENNY: I promise I'd keep it miserable.

ACT ONE 23

TOM: No, Lenny.

(MA *finds box of mementos.*)

MA: Here's my box o' keepsakes. Ain't no use to us so's I'll leave it behind.

TOM: Ma, you love that stuff.

MA: No time fer the past now, Tommy. We got to look to the future. You and Lenny go help Pa. I'd like to look through these things one last time.

TOM: Okay, Ma.

(LENNY *and* TOM *exit.* MA *sits down with the box of mementos and begins to remove items one by one. The first item is an old photograph; the second is a pair of baby shoes; the third is a huge Oklahoma Sooners foam-rubber hat,* MA *puts the hat on, does the "Wave," and sits back down; the last item is a T-shirt, the front of which reads:* MY SON WENT TO PRISON. MA *flips the shirt over to reveal the back, which reads:* AND ALL I GOT WAS THIS LOUSY T-SHIRT. MA *wipes her tearful eyes with the shirt.*)

(*Offstage we hear a loud pig squeal.* LENNY, PA *and* TOM *enter.*)

PA: Well, we's done, Ma.

MA: Thought you was gonna shoot that pig.

PA: Did'n have to. 'Fore I could raise my gun, Lenny gave it a good-bye hug, an' that were enough to do the job. Is you ready, Ma?

MA: Ready as I'll ever be. (*Bravely*) You boys load the rest o' these boxes on the truck. Pa, go strap Granma in an' git some water. We's goin' to California!

(MA, PA *and* TOM *strike a tableau pose and stare out hopefully to horizon.* LENNY *follows them at first, but then begins to glance around confusedly.*)

(*Lights fade. End of Scene One*)

Scene Two

(Setting: A small roadside cafe. GUS is seated at the counter talking to MAE. AL is heard working in the kitchen.)

GUS: ...then the priest says, "Well, if you're the rabbi, then where in heck is the golf pro?!"

MAE: *(Laughing)* We sure have missed you around here, Gus. How long you been back on this route, anyhow?

GUS: Been about a week now. I was hauling cottage cheese out in Nebraska, but it didn't pay off.

MAE: When did you get a refrigerator truck?

GUS: I didn't. It was milk when I left Oregon. That's why they got me back here on 66. Besides, I missed your hospitality, Mae. How about a slice of your best pie and a cup of java.

MAE: We have banana cream, pineapple cream, chocolate cream and apple.

GUS: What's that big fluffy one?

MAE: Oh that isn't pie, that's a dust ball. They blow around here like tumbleweed. Gets in everything.

GUS: Gimme a doughnut Mae.

MAE: *(Giving him doughnuts)* Here you go, Honey. They're mighty small. I shouldn't do this, but here's an extra one.

GUS: Now that's hospitality.

AL: Why don't you just give him the whole damn dozen, Mae.

GUS: What's with Al?

MAE: The cafe's in a pinch right now. Ever since those Okies started clogging 66, all the truckers are taking the bypass.

ACT ONE

GUS: Don't those shitheel Okies stop to eat?

MAE: Oh, sure, they stop. Come in here, whole family of fourteen taking up a booth, ordering just water. Then they eat all the catsup, the creamers, the sugar packets; pull out a dried up road turtle and use up the good steak sauce on it! Then they shower in the bathroom and leave.

GUS: Jesus! Al, you must be losing your shirt.

MAE: Would you like to try one of our new maple logs?

AL: Between those traveling shitheels, and Mae's two-for-one give away policy, I might as well close shop now.

GUS: What makes those migrants think things are any better in California anyway? The way I hear it, jobs are just as scarce there as anywhere.

MAE: *(Grabbing catsup and sugar from counter)* Uh oh, stow the 57 Al, Okies at three o'clock.

(MA *and* PA *enter.*)

PA: 'Scuse me, ma'am...

(LENNY *runs in, bumping into* MA *and* PA.)

PA: *(Gives* LENNY *stare, turns to* MAE*)* Can we git some water fer our truck?

MAE: Sure, around the side. Help yourself.

LENNY: Can I get it, Pa Joad? Can I? Huh? Can I—

PA: Just get it!

(LENNY *exits.*)

PA: I swear Ma, if 'n jus' one more time I had to hear him sing, "A Hundred Bottles Of Beer On The Wall...."

MA: Have patience, Pa. He's simple.

PA: Well, I wisht we'd at least got us a Travel Yahtzee. And somethin' fer Granma, too. She's been so quiet 'n all. *(Turns to leave)*

MA: Pa, I been meanin' to tell ya somethin' 'bout Granma. *(To* MAE*)* Ma'am, mind if we set in a booth fer a spell?

MAE: Sure.

AL: No!

MAE: No.

MA: Granma's dead, Pa. Travelin' were jus' too much fer a woman o' her years.

PA: Oh, Ma...

MA: She passed on when we stopped by that river to fix the flat.

PA: Ma, we had that flat tire three weeks ago.

MA: I know'd I should a tol' you sooner, but, in the back of the truck, she was the only thing 'tween me and Lenny. Besides, I knew we had to keep going, to git to California. We can bury her there where it's nice and green, Pa. She'd like that.

(An uncomfortable silence)

MAE: Uh... Gus, more coffin? Coffee!

GUS: No thanks. *(To the Joads)* Um, you folks heading to California?

PA: Yes sir.

GUS: Might want to turn back now. Ain't no work out there.

MA: *(Taking out flyer)* But we got this here flyer, says they's lookin' fer pickers.

GUS: I've seen those all over. They need a hundred men, so they print five thousand flyers, and two

ACT ONE 27

thousand men show up for the job. Just look at the roads. They're clogged with folks looking for work.

AL: Hey Mae, it's ten after the hour. Turn on the traffic report.

RADIO VOICEOVER: ...From highway 66 to interstate 80, all roads are still clogged by them damn Okies. It's two days to the bypass, and three weeks to junction 14. Your listening to K-R-O-P, All-Farming Radio. Five minutes of music and fifty-five minutes of pure Krop. And now this...

RADIO AD: *(Different voice)* Peaches, peaches, peaches! Out of work? Run off your land? Or just looking for some extra cash? Well, look no further than California, because Crazy Curly is HIRING! Yes, Crazy Curly's Pickin' Plantation wants you. Whether you're an Arkie, an Okie, or genetically pokey, Curly is offering one dollar a bushel! That's one whole dollar! We've got to be CRAZY to pay a dollar a bushel! But that's not all! You get free board, showers, and health insurance! Yes, you heard right! Plus, free Sunday paper and continental breakfast included. Look at the facts and you'll agree, WE GOTTA BE NUTS!!! So come to Crazy Curly's Pickin' Plantation where our motto is, "You're pickin', we're grinnin'."

(MAE *turns radio off.*)

PA: See Ma, there's work to be found. And they give ya free board, so's we can 'ventually build that house you been pinin' fer.

(TOM *enters.*)

TOM: Pa, where did we pack the toolkit?

PA: Right under the front seat — what's the matter, Tommy? Did Mister Monkeywrench bust my truck?

TOM: Well, actually, Pa, it's just a little, minor, kind of—

(LENNY *enters, carrying the radiator from the Joad's truck.*)

LENNY: I think I found a leak, Joad.

PA: Gol dang it, Lenny!!

TOM: I'll take care of it, Pa. Lenny, you stay in here and keep out of trouble.

(TOM *exits.*)

LENNY: (*Looking off*) Ooo, jukebox!

AL, MA, MAE & PA: Don't touch that!

MA: We'll be leavin' soon enough, Lenny.

MAE: Cute boy you got there.

MA: He ain't mine, I swear he ain't. Ma'am, 'fore we go, could you see your way to sellin' us a loaf of bread?

MAE: This isn't a grocery store. We don't sell loaves. How about a sandwich? We got good sandwiches.

MA: We can't afford no san'wich.

GUS: Aw, Mae. Sell her the bread.

MAE: But the bread truck don't come 'til Thursday.

GUS: Go on Mae.

PA: We'd be beholdin'.

MAE: All right. A loaf of bread is fifteen cents.

MA: We can only afford ten cents fer bread, we done budgeted fer this trip pretty tight. Could you see to cuttin' off ten cents worth?

MAE: I can't cut it. Who would buy the rest of the loaf?

GUS: Why doesn't Al throw it into his stuffing?

MAE: That's cornbread stuffing, and this is wheat.

MA: Can't you use it fer your san'wiches?

ACT ONE   29

MAE: If I sold you two-thirds of the loaf, I would have to slice the rest mighty thin to get an even amount of slices.

PA: I don't figger.

MAE: Look, I get thirty-four slices a loaf. That's seventeen sandwiches. Ten cents is two-thirds of a loaf, or twenty-two-point-seven slices. That leaves me eleven-point-three slices, which makes five sandwiches with one slice-point-three left over. And I can't use that.

GUS: Wait a minute Mae. If you got eleven-point-three slices left, and you cut them diagonally twice into triangles, you'd have thirty-four triangles and that would make seventeen finger sandwiches.

MAE: Gus, you idiot. Thrity-three of them triangles would be isosceles, and the point-three triangle would be equal at sides A and B only. Nice finger sandwich.

AL: Look Mae, just make the five sandwiches, take the one-point-three leftovers, cut the one in half and you got one-half a triple decker club.

MAE: Al, whose gonna buy one half a triple club?

AL: I will! Just sell 'em the damn loaf, and get 'em out of here!!

MAE: Fine. Here you go. *(Slams loaf onto counter)*

PA: And we're much obliged Ma'am. *(Turning to leave)* Let's go, Lenny. Lenny, what are you staring at? Oh, candy, huh?

LENNY: *(Staring into candy jars on counter)* Can we git some?

MA: I don't know, Lenny. Ma'am, is that penny candy?

MAE: That candy? Uh... No. That candy is...two for a penny.

MA: Two fer a penny...hmmm.

(MA *and* PA *step aside to confer.*)

GUS: *(To* MAE*)* That ain't two-for-a-penny candy.

MAE: What's it to you?

GUS: Those are five-cent candies.

MAE: All right. Maybe I do got a soft spot for these folks. Big deal.

(MA *and* PA *return.*)

MA: Okay. We'll take fifteen dollars worth of the candy...an' lessee, a carton of Chesterfields...

PA: Copy of Humor Down on the Farm.

MA: And twenty Lotto quick picks.

LENNY: How 'bout something fer Granma. Seein' how she's been so quiet lately.

PA: Granma, right...oh, give us three gross of them pine tree auto fresheners!

MAE: I'll write this up. You might want to pull your truck around to the loading dock.

MA: Thank you ma'am.

PA: Let's go Lenny.

(LENNY, MA *and* PA *exit.*)

MAE: Go ahead Al, tell me I'm a pushover.

AL: No, you're not a pushover, Mae. You're unemployed! We lost a hundred-and-thirty-five dollars on penny candy alone.

GUS: *(Tosses money on counter)* Gotta go, Mae. *(He exits quickly.)*

AL: Hey, Mae, you're ride's leaving.

MAE: Damn Okies.

(Lights fade. End of Scene Two)

ACT ONE

Scene Three

(Setting: A California border station. The lights come up to reveal LENNY, MA, PA *and* TOM *standing before the building. All but* TOM *have clothespins on their noses.)*

PA: *(Gesturing out)* Look ever'body, California! Ain't she beautiful?

LENNY: We made it, Joad.

MA: First thing we gotta do is bury Granma. *(Takes off clothespin)* Least now she can git buried in a nice green place. *(Looking around)* What is this place?

TOM: Border station, Ma. They're gonna want to inspect the truck.

MA: They can't Tommy. Granma's back there. They'll stop us fer sure. Can't we just pile back in the truck and blow right past 'em?

*(*GUARD *enters from the station and approaches the* JOADS.*)*

GUARD: All right you Okies, stand away from the vehicle.

PA: *(Staring off)* Look, grapes! *(He runs off toward grapes.)*

GUARD: *(Yelling off to* PA*)* Hey, you, don't go past that chain link fence! All right, let's get through this —

MA: Listen, sir, we got us a sick woman in the back of the truck, we got to git to a doctor right away.

GUARD: State law, ma'am. I have to check your belongings.

TOM: We ain't got nothin'.

GUARD: Nothing to declare?

TOM: No sir.

GUARD: I bet.

TOM: I swear.

GUARD: *(Reading off clipboard)* No fruit?

TOM: No.

GUARD: Plants or seeds?

TOM: No.

GUARD: Firearms, fireworks?

TOM: No.

GUARD: Condor traps, med flies, tropical birds or Christmas trees?

TOM: Christmas trees?!

GUARD: Any vegetables?

LENNY: Does granma count?

MA: Look, sir, we ain't got nothin' but a washtub full of Gummi Bears an' a very sickly woman who gots to see a doctor right away.

GUARD: Well, she'll have to wait. I need to check the back of the truck. *(He exits to inspect truck.)*

MA: Oh, Tom...

TOM: It's all right, Ma.

GUARD: *(Offstage)* My God!! *(Entering)* That truck smells like a godamn pine forest. You sure you're not transportin' Christmas trees?

(They shake their heads in response.)

GUARD: All right. County Hospital is eight miles up the road.

MA: Thank you, sir!

GUARD: And I strongly advise you to stop by the Twinkle-Kwik car wash before you hit town. Now get the hell out of here.

TOM: Pa! Let's go. The guard says we can go!

ACT ONE 33

PA: *(Entering with grape crate)* Tommy! These is the best grapes I ever et. We ought to settle right here. I wonder who's grapes these is? Maybe this orchard is Crazy Curly's!

TOM: Reckon I don't know, Pa.

LENNY: *(Reading sign on grape crate)* Oh, it ain't Crazy Curly's orchard, Joad. It belongs to someone with the initials D D T.

PA: Well, they's good, heh, heh... Funny after-burn, though.

(PA collapses. TOM supports him.)

MA: Pa! Pa! Is you all right?

PA: Don't think so. Looks like I done bought the farm this time...

LENNY: *(Excitedly grabs PA)* Did ya buy one with rabbits on it?

PA: Gol dang it, Lenny! *(He has a coughing fit.)* Kfgh! Kfgh!

MA: Pa!

PA: Now, now, it's all right. All the sore luck and odds 'ginst the family not makin' it is behind us now. All I ever wanted was to git to California, and I'm here, with my family... God bless you all. *(He dies.)*

MA: Pa! PA!!

TOM: It's all right, Ma. *(Pulling MA off PA)* Pa got the one thing he always wanted. He made it to California. He made it, Ma.

(Long pause as GUARD slowly walks up behind them.)

GUARD: Hate to bring this up, 'specially if you're a stickler about these things, but this here is just the border crossing. *(Pointing)* The state line starts down there, at the bottom of this ravine. *(He exits.)*

(The family pauses, looking reverently at each other as they realize what they must do. Slowly they start to kick and roll PA *toward the ravine.)*

(Lights fade.)

END OF ACT ONE

ACT TWO

(Setting: The interior of a bunkhouse on a fruit farm. Lights half up as Casy *stumbles in, clutching his head, and falls to the floor.* Candy *enters, helps* Casy *to the bed, and exits.* Casy *is passed out on the bed, facing the wall.* Ma *and* Tom *enter, carrying empty buckets.)*

Ma: Bunkhouse 16. This is our'n, Tommy. See, they even dropped off our belongin's fer us.

Tom: At's the least they could do. Why we weren't through Crazy Curly's front gate more'n five minutes 'fore they had us out in the orchard workin' harder'n a one-legged man in a sack race. Wisht they'd put me on the same crew as Lenny; he might git lost on his own.

Ma: He'll be fine. I pinned our cabin number on his overalls. *(Looking about the room)* Once we spruce up in here, it'll be a nice little home fer the three of us.

Tom: *(Lighting lantern, notices* Casy*)* Four, Ma. Looks like we got us a bunkmate.

Ma: I was hopin' fer a single family unit, but we'll make do.

Tom: *(Looking at* Casy*)* Looks mighty beat up.

Ma: *(Looking about the room)* I've seen worse.

Tom: What'ya think we oughta do?

Ma: Git right to work. It ain't nothin' a little elbow grease an' a broomstick won't take care of.

TOM: Wha'?

MA: Granma always said ain't nothin' lifts a sperit like a good sweepin' out.

TOM: Take it from a convict, Ma, it won't help the guy.

MA: Guy?!

TOM: I'll bet he's the one we seen git beat up fer makin' a ruckus at the front gate. Wonder what that was all about, anyways? Hey mister. *(Goes to wake* CASY*)*

MA: Tommy, you keep clear o' him. If'n he's a troublemaker, I don't want you bein' no part of it. After travelin' two thousand miles through mountain and desert, losin' Granma and Pa on the way, havin' nothin' to eat but salt pork and penny candy, reachin' California to land back breakin' work in the swelterin' heat. After all that, I ain't gonna let you git mixed up in no trouble, and ruin the best summer we's had in twenty years.

TOM: Ma, I ain't lookin' fer trouble. It's jus' he's been beat up, an' it ain't like no Joad to walk away from a guy in need.

MA: I don't want nothin' happenin' to you, Tommy. We's the only Joads left.

CASY: *(Awakening)* Joads?... You folks say you was Joads?

TOM: Well I'll be damned if'n it ain't Jim Casy! Ma, that there's the preacher I done told you about, in the flesh.

CASY: I told you I ain't a preacher! And as a result I ain't been in the flesh goin' on six months now. Pardon me, Ma'am.

MA: I remember you. I still got the tattoo on my ass from pentecost.

TOM: Casy, how'd you end up out here?

ACT TWO

CASY: Well, I been followin' my new callin. Walkin' the back roads and riverbanks of this land, listenin' to what the common folk had to say. One day I was wanderin' through some desert hills, about half-crazy with hunger and thirst, and I come upon a sign.

MA: Were it a sign from God, preacher?

CASY: No, it were a sign said "HOLLYWOOD," with letters taller'n a circus freak. That's when I realized that I'd up and walked clear to California. Hell, beat you out here to boot.

TOM: Yeah, our truck is slower'n a one-toothed man in a corn-eatin' contest.

CASY: Seein's yer here, I assumes you got run off yer land.

TOM: We'd a stayed and fought. But Pa figgered California were the place we ought ta be, so we loaded up the truck and we moved out here to find work. 'Sides, Pa always said a warm climate'd be good fer a man's health.

CASY: How is yer Pa?

TOM: Dead. Got kilt just short a the state line.

CASY: Homocide?

TOM: No, insecticide. Lost Granma on the way, too, but we kept a goin'. Casy, can't help but noticin'... We seen a man git beat up by the front gate, an' that bump on your head there don't look like no chigger bite.

CASY: Yeah, it were me. Popped me good.

MA: Let's see 'er.

(CASY *shows his head wound.*)

MA: My lord, Casy, you needs attendin' to. Tommy, git me some iodine an' I'll clean that up.

(TOM *gets iodine and a cloth from belongings and gives them to* MA, *who tends to* CASY.)

TOM: What the hell was goin' on, Casy?

CASY: I was jus' speakin' through the chain link to the folks on the road. Tellin' 'em about the way things is here in the camp, and figgerin' a way to change 'em fer the better.

MA: They's nothin' here needs changin' if'n you ask me. We's gettin' a dollar a box fer the peaches we pick, and they give us a place to stay. Even puttin' on a square dance tonight fer recreations.

CASY: Things here ain't what they seems, Mrs Joad. Sure, it's likable on the surface, but if'n you look closer, you'll see there's a evil here, same kinda evil run you off yer farm.

TOM: Casy, you got me more confused than a one-eyed man at a 3-D movie. Ain't they got work here?

CASY: Sure, they got work. Got work fer maybe two hundred men. But the owners know damn well that they's two thousand men would be glad to take them jobs. So they print up a big batch of flyers an' run annoyin' ads on the radio to attract suckers down on their luck. 'Fore you know it, they got ten men fer ever' job. Now they can pay what they want, an' I can tell you they don't mean to pay much.

MA: Still, it's money. Money enough to spend on meat at the comp'ny store. That's what we's havin' tonight soon's we git paid. Big slab o' meat. You're welcome to share it with us, Casy.

TOM: Won't be a minute too soon, neither. I'd jus' as soon's starve to death as eat another one of them godamn Smarties.

ACT TWO

CASY: And that comp'ny store, that's another trap. They charges you double what you pay in town, and makes you bag your own.

MA: Well, we'll make do.

(LENNY *enters, carrying a small bag of peaches. Not seeing* TOM *or* MA, *he approaches* CASY.)

LENNY: You seen the Joads?

TOM: Lenny, where you been?

LENNY: Got lost.

MA: But I pinned the cabin number on you so's you'd find us.

LENNY: *(Looking down at his number)* I looked and looked, Mrs Ma, but there weren't no cabin ninety one. *(Giving bag to* MA*)* Here, I sneaked out some peaches from the field.

MA: Well, that's right good thinkin' Lenny. *(Looks in bag)* Kinda soft ain't they?

LENNY: Had to sneak 'em out in my shoes.

MA: I'll git to peelin' 'em.

LENNY: *(Seeing* CASY*)* Say, ain't you the preacher?

CASY, MA & TOM: He/I ain't a preacher!

LENNY: Really? You look just like a preacher we met in Oklahoma. One Joad said were a lunatic pervert who couldn't be trusted and who—

TOM: Nah, nah, nah, this here's Casy. Old friend of the family.

LENNY: What happened to your head, Casy?

CASY: Got beat up fer speakin' the truth. Jus' tellin' a couple fellas I didn't think the peach basket rental fee were fair, an' the owner come along and smashed my head plum to squash.

MA: Crazy Curly done this to you?

CASY: That's right. They don't call her Crazy Curly fer nothin'. Why, she's just about the meanest person you ever did see. Some say it's her hair makes her crazy; say it's curled up so tight that it's squeezin' the livin' Jesus out of her brain. Wears one leather glove on her right hand, too. A fella tol' me that Curly stitched a handful of little rocks into that glove. Likes to use it on the fellas she picks fights with, 'specially fellas who're bigger'n she is.

LENNY: I'm a big fella, Joad.

TOM: I know you are, Lenny, an' I don't want you messin' with this Curly none. If you do, all of us is gonna git the heave-ho.

LENNY: I don't want no trouble, Joad.

TOM: You just keep away from her, Lenny. She comes at you, you back off. Don't give her no chance to git near you. You understand?

LENNY: Yes, Joad.

(The door swings open and CURLY bursts in. Her hair is a huge tangle of tight curls. She is wearing a holstered pistol, one leather glove, and is carrying a whip.)

CURLY: Evenin', slugs!

LENNY: *(Pointing at CURLY)* Joad, that must be...

TOM: *(Under his breath)* Shut up, Lenny!

CURLY: I've come to pay a call on the troublemaker. *(Approaching CASY)* You had enough time to think, troublemaker? About that little discussion we had this morning? The one about you preaching the gospel according to Lenin?

CASY: I've been thinkin' plenty.

ACT TWO 41

CURLY: That's good. Maybe you can think up a way to pay for the repairs on that fence I raked your face across. Of course, sometimes it's easier to think when you're sitting down.

(CURLY *punches* CASY *and shoves him onto the bed. She turns toward the others.)*

CURLY: You slugs new to the ranch?

MA: We's the Joads from Salisaw, Oklahoma.

CURLY: *(Approaching* MA*)* And I'm Crazy Curly. Hell, I must be crazy to have let in the likes of you, granma. You look like something right out of one of them W P A photographs.

MA: Don't worry none about me. I can earn my keep. I've worked hard all my life, tillin' and harvestin' on forty acres of arid soil, raisin' up a fambly good an' proud—

CURLY: *(Interrupting)* Spare me the details, granma. If I've heard that hard-luck Okie story once I've heard it a thousand times.

TOM: Maybe you never heard it told right.

CURLY: Oh, got us a smart guy here, do we? Well, smart guy, you ever done any hard labor? Let me see your hands. *(He grabs* TOM's *hands, looks them over, then places his right hand into thumb-wrestling position.)* Ready smart guy? One. Two. Three!

(They thumb-wrestle, and CURLY *pins his thumb down hard.)*

TOM: Aghhh!!

LENNY: Hey, let go of him!

*(*LENNY *lunges at* CURLY. TOM *moves to push* LENNY *away and holds him back.)*

CURLY: What's that, junior? (*Approaching* LENNY, *who nervously looks away*) Look at me when I'm talkin' to you, junior! (*Close to his face*) Or are you trying to avoid looking at something in particular? Maybe something in the vicinity of the top of my head?!

TOM: He didn't say nothin'.

CURLY: Let the big guy talk!

TOM: S'pose'n he don't want to talk?

CURLY: By God, he'll talk when he's spoke to. What business is it of yours, anyhow?

TOM: Him and me's travelin' together.

CURLY: Oh, so it's that way.

TOM: What way?

CURLY: You know what I mean.

TOM: 'Fraid I don't.

CURLY: You know, two grown men, traveling together, talking for one another...sleeping in the same quarters...

(*Everyone looks puzzled.*)

CURLY: Maybe...once in a while going to a Judy Garland movie...

TOM: What the hell you gettin' at?

CURLY: Why don't you let the big guy talk?!

TOM: He can talk, if he's got somethin' to say.

LENNY: (*In a frightened voice*) We don't want no trouble, Harpo...er, sir...ma'am!

CURLY: (*Draws gun and points it at* LENNY) That's strike one, junior. (*Turns gun to* MA *and* TOM) But, I didn't come here to B S with you Salisaw slugs. I'm here to tell you the Rules of the Ranch. (*Puts gun back in holster*) So listen up good all of you. Rule Number One: No bruised fruit. Rule Number Two: No talking

ACT TWO 43

on company time. Rule Number Three: No smoking, littering, or radio playing. Please do not lean against the doors. And Rule Number Four, my personal favorite: Crazy Curly's Pickin' Plantation reserves the right to change any and all of the above rules without notice. You follow these rules and there won't be no trouble. But don't ever forget that outside my ranch right now I got folks lining up ten miles deep hoping just for a chance to sneak barebelly over a field of barbed wire so they can bribe a guard to let 'em enter a lottery for the jobs you got. *(He turns to leave.)*

MA: Hold on a minute. When is it we git paid?

CURLY: Oh, I'll pay you right now. Let me see your receipt from the foreman.

(MA *hands* CURLY *receipt. She begins figuring pay.)*

CURLY: All right...you picked twenty boxes of peaches, so that's twenty times...an' carry the two...that comes to...one dollar even.

MA: One dollar?! I thought they done told us we git a dollar a box.

CURLY: That was this morning, granny, before trading in peach futures opened up. Since then we've had a slight adjustment on the downward side.

TOM: That ain't right.

MA: *(Holding* TOM *back)* Tommy, you keep clear of this. Even one dollar is a dollar more'n what we got now. *(To* CURLY*)* We'll take it.

CURLY: At least one of you damn Okies got sense. Here you go, one dollar even.

MA: What kinda money is this?

CURLY: That's one dollar in Curly Coins. You can redeem them at Crazy Curly's Country Kitchen and Smokehouse.

CASY: Way that store's set up, a dollar won't hardly buy you a trial size Slim-Jim.

CURLY: *(Crossing to* CASY*)* Listen here, troublemaker, when I want some lip from you I'll get religion!

*(*CURLY *slugs* CASY*. He falls back.)*

MA: Leave him be!

CURLY: What was that, granny? *(He crosses to* MA *and grabs her by the collar.)* I don't think I heard you quite right...

LENNY: Stop it! Stop it! Leave Ma alone!!

*(*LENNY *grabs* CURLY*'s fist. In agony,* CURLY *slowly sinks to her knees as* LENNY *continues to squeeze her fist.)*

MA & TOM: Lenny, Let go! Let go of her hand!

(Keep up until LENNY *releases* CURLY*'s fist)*

*(*LENNY *looks around in confusion before realizing his actions. He lets go of* CURLY*'s fist and she collapses, rubbing her injured hand.)*

LENNY: But, Joad, she was hurtin' Ma. It weren't fair! She's nothin' but a big bully, a big mean bully with silly-lookin' hair!

*(*CANDY *bursts through door.)*

CANDY: Um...don't mean to interrupt.

CURLY: What?!

CANDY: The band just arrived. They need to know where the outlets are.

CURLY: All right. *(Pointing at* LENNY*)* No one touches me like that. I'll remember what you done. I'll remember you good.

*(*CURLY *exits,* CANDY *pauses at the door.)*

CANDY: *(To* CASY*)* I'll be right back. *(Exits)*

ACT TWO

CASY: Do you see what we's up against, Tom? Us workers don't stand a chance against owners like Curly. Not lessin' we organize.

CANDY: *(Poking head in door)* Helloooo. May I...uh...?

CASY: Come on in, Candy.

CANDY: Evenin'. Evenin', Ma'am. *(To* CASY*)* Are we safe?

CASY: Yeah, these folks is all right.

*(*CANDY *and* CASY *share a secret union handshake.)*

CASY: How's it going fer the square dance tonight?

CANDY: Good. We snuck in two truckloads of workers from Salinas, and they's with us. Got a couple a union organizers from down state too.

CASY: Hot damn! We's ready to turn this here square dance into the biggest labor sign-up since the Czar took a powder.

CANDY: They's just one problem, though. Hate to bring it up... *(Pulls flyers out of bag)* These Union picket flyers you wrote. They's a word misspellt on 'em.

CASY: Well, one misspellt word can't hurt. What word is it?

CANDY: Union. Them folks from Salinas thinks they's here to pick onions.

CASY: We're jus' gonna hav'ta fix 'em, tha's all.

CANDY: Okay. I brought a pencil. Uh...mind if I work here? Fourteen kids in the bunkhouse...you know...

CASY: Sure, that's fine. *(To* TOM*)* Tom, come here a minute. Tom Joad, this here's Candy. He's a foreman here, but he's workin' to help us unionize.

TOM: Pleased to meet ya.

CANDY: Uh...hello.

CASY: And that's Mrs. Joad, an' Lenny.

MA: Lenny ain't mine.

CASY: Tom. See what I have in my hand? The birth of a union, fresh off a mimeograph machine. Here! Smell 'em.

(CANDY, CASY *and* TOM *take a long, satisfying whiff of mimeograph odor and let out a sigh: "Ahhhh".)*

CANDY: I best get started on these.

(CASY *gives* CANDY *the stack of flyers, then turns and hands one to* LENNY.)

CANDY: Nice to have you with us, Tom Joad.

MA: He ain't with ya. He don't want no part of your kind o' trouble.

CASY: Union needs men like you, Tom. A man who believes in himself. A man who'll stick to his convictions. A man with a prison record.

TOM: Aw Casy, I'd like to help ya, but I ain't even sure what a union is.

LENNY: Union? Hell, I ain't sure what an onion is.

MA: He's right. All across the country, he's been callin' 'em "stinky peaches."

CASY: *(Pulling* TOM *aside)* It's like this, Tom. People's always frettin' 'cause they's powerless to help themselves. Well by themselves they'll stay that way. But if'n enough people starts workin' together, workin' as a team, why that team can change things. Say they want to work us eighteen hours a day, or cut the bushel price, or make us wear stupid lookin' hairnets, then we could band together and force 'em to treat us fair.

TOM: How?

CASY: By strikin' 'em!

ACT TWO 47

TOM: With a shovel?

CASY: No! With the combined— *(Turns to* TOM*)* actually that's not a bad idea—but first, by the combined convictions of ever' worker in the camp. And once the camp is unified, we can git ever' worker in California to join in, formin' 'em into what we calls a "local," and each and ever' man'll be proud to wear his union jacket or lapel pin. We'll have big national meetin's ever' year in Las Vegas, paid fer by what we call "dues." The union will give folk like us a voice, Tom, and that voice'll be yellin' equal work fer equal wages. Equal work fer equal wages!

LENNY: Will that work?

TOM: What do you mean, Lenny?

LENNY: Well, supposin' ya had a real busy rabbit, and a lazy rabbit, and ya feeds them both the same. Now the busy rabbit is fun to play with, but the lazy rabbit just lays around stinkin' up the hutch. Well, wouldn't ya think the busy rabbit would see that he'd git fed the same if'n he too jus' laid around the hutch? And wouldn't that make you hav'ta kill the lazy rabbit so's that wouldn't happen?

TOM: Lenny, are you sayin' Casy's wrong? That if'n all folks is paid equal, and runs the companies and owns the land, that the competitive incentive will be lost, an' tha' one day it'll all collapse because of some innate human desire fer a market driven economy?

LENNY: No, I'm sayin' I kill'd my rabbit, Joad.

CASY: I ain't talkin' 'bout rabbits, Lenny. I'm talkin' 'bout workers, an' how they's treated.

TOM: And how they need's a voice....

MA: We gotta keep the fambly together, Tommy. If'n you start rockin' the boat now, there'll be trouble fer sure. I don't like it, Tommy, not one bit.

TOM: But Ma, we don't got nothin' here. No money, no food.

MA: We got these four peaches. It may not be much, but we been through worse. We seen drought and locusts destroy our crops; we seen a year's hard worked wiped out by floods, disease and little league games. Think about it, Tommy, we just traveled across this land eatin' nothin' but pig and Pez. If four peaches is all we got, even if they's smooshed up and smellin' like socks, then we should give thanks and try to enjoy 'em.

TOM: You're right, Ma.

MA: They's ready now. You men come and eat.

(CASY, LENNY and TOM *sit down at the table.* CANDY *approaches the table.*)

MA: Candy, I'd ask you to join us but we's only got the four peaches.

CANDY: Oh...that's all right. You go ahead and eat. I'll just sit over here an' correct the rest of these flyers.

TOM: Have you and your family et already?

CANDY: No, but that's... I'm fine.

MA: Well if'n yer hungry, maybe we could share a little.

CANDY: No, no, don't worry about me none.

MA: Well all right then. Casy? You wanna drop yer britches and say grace fer us?

TOM: Ma, let's just say grace in our own heads.

(*In their silence, we hear the sound of* CANDY's *stomach growling.*)

CASY: Is that you, Candy?

CANDY: It's nothin'. Go on and eat.

ACT TWO

(Stomach growl)

MA: Candy, I'd find it a bit more appetizing if'n you'd join us.

CANDY: Thank you, ma'am, but I couldn't eat supper knowin' that my family's sittin' back in our bunkhouse starvin'.

(Louder stomach growl)

TOM: Well, that's enough fer me.

CASY: Same here.

MA: I guess. Here Candy. I want you to take these peaches home right now.

CANDY: That's kind but I...

MA: Now I don't want no back talk, you jus' take 'em and git.

(The sound of a triangle ringing offstage is heard.)

CASY: There's the bell signalin' the start o' the square dance. *(To* CANDY*)* We'll take care of the flyers, you just git on home and see to it your little ones git fed.

CANDY: *(Taking peaches)* Well, I don't know how to thank you.

MA: Just as long as yer family gits to eat today.

CANDY: 'Course we don't...well, we don't need plates.

MA: No, you take ours.

CANDY: I don't want to impose or nothin'.

MA: No, you take 'em, and the silver, too.

CANDY: If'n it's all right. And the salt, please.

MA: Oh, yes...

CANDY: And the table cloth would be nice.

MA: Now—

CANDY: And if a couple o' you men would help with the table, we could....

MA: Git out!

CANDY: Are those curtains yours?

MA: Git the hell out of my bunkhouse!!

CANDY: *(Backing out door)* Yeah...okay...I'll see you at the meetin'. Much obliged for every...yeah...bye.

TOM: See, Ma? Casy's right. If'n us workers don't take a stand, we's all gonna end up grovelin' like Candy.

MA: Don't say that, Tommy! Union's is for folks who can't provide for themselves, an' we ain't sunk that low yet. We'll scare up dinner somehow.

LENNY: Oh, I almost forgot! I also smuggled out a yam in my pants. *(Searches through his overalls)*

MA: *(Slow take)* Tommy, let's go organize us a Union!

CASY: That's the sperit! Okay, now our secret sign is a red bandana. Wear it like this.

(CASY *hands* MA *and* TOM *red bandanas, and ties one around his neck.)*

LENNY: Can I have a yellow one, Casy? I want a yellow bandana.

TOM: Uh, Lenny, we need you to stay inside. There could be trouble at the dance and it's best you're not near it.

LENNY: I wouldn't fast dance, Joad.

TOM: No. You stay right here and don't git into no trouble. Ma, Casy, let's go.

(CASY, MA *and* TOM *exit to the union square dance.* LENNY *sits on the bed and pulls a mouse out of his pocket.)*

LENNY: Be very quiet, okay, mouse? There could be trouble at the dance and it's best you're not near it.

ACT TWO

'Member what happened in Weed? Do you? What happened, 'cause I got no idea.

(Noise offstage)

LENNY: Shh. Someone's comin'! Quick, hide under the bed.

(LENNY *puts mouse under the bed. After a few seconds, the* "SNAP" *of a mousetrap is heard.* LENNY *leans over to look under the bed while the door opens and* CURLY *enters. The sound of music from the dance outside is heard faintly.)*

CURLY: Evening, peelhead. Don't feel like dancin'?

LENNY: Nothin'.

CURLY: You're awful squirrely for a big guy. Do I scare ya?

LENNY: *(Scared)* No. *(He looks around uncomfortably.)*

CURLY: Then look at me when I'm talkin' to you! *(Close to his face)* Look at me! LOOK AT ME!

(LENNY *suddenly looks at* CURLY.*)*

CURLY: What are you lookin' at?! Wouldn't be admirin' my coif, would ya?

LENNY: *(Looking away)* I wasn't lookin' at nothin'. I was jus' hearin' the music. I like the banjos.

CURLY: I like the banjos! I like the banjos! Godamn, I know your type. You'd rather be sacheyin' 'round a hay dance than findin' yerself alone with a real woman!

LENNY: It's jus' that...Joad and Casy says that...

CURLY: What do they say?

LENNY: They say you're a bad news and a ball buster and I best not look at ya or talk to ya or nothin' and that you're the kind a' skirt that's goin' to git us all in trouble, like the one in Weed, the one I— *(He slaps his hand over his mouth.)*

CURLY: *(Smilin')* The one you what? Huh? *(Pause)* Well, spit in a silo, you got yourself a way with ladies, don't ya.

LENNY: Kinda. But I ain't s'posed to say nothin' about it.

CURLY: So I bet you're wanting to join the party then, huh? Maybe pick up the wife of some drunk hand and get her in the loft to buck the barley?

LENNY: No, no! I promised Joad! I won't do nothin' bad. I'm stayin' right put, Mrs Curly! Don't make me!

CURLY: Okay, forget the dance. You can stay right where you are, Lenny, alone in the bunk house with me.

LENNY: Uh...

CURLY: Lenny?

LENNY: Yeah, Mrs Curly?

CURLY: Nobody lays a hand on me like you did.

LENNY: I'm really sorry, all I was doin' was—

CURLY: No! I liked it. But you're the only guy I ever had in camp with the stones to do it. And you ain't afraid to talk square. Tell me somethin'...

LENNY: Okay. Joad and I are goin' to git a farm someday, with rabbits and chickens and—

CURLY: No, tell me somethin' I ask! Be honest, too. Lenny, how do the workers in camp feel about me?

LENNY: Fer honest?

CURLY: Yeah.

LENNY: They hate your stinking guts.

CURLY: Well sure, but aside from that, what are they saying?

ACT TWO

LENNY: I only remember the stuff about your guts. Sorry, Mrs Curly.

CURLY: And quit callin' me that.

LENNY: Mrs Curly?

CURLY: I ain't Mrs Curly.

LENNY: Mr Curly?

CURLY: No!

LENNY: Curl-lew. Curl-lay. Curl-low...

CURLY: It's Curly, you idiot! Plain Curly. Look at my damn hair, what else are you going to call me?! Humidity gets above thirty, I presto into Bride of Frankenstein.

LENNY: I git it! Curly 'cause o' your hair.

CURLY: It's 'cause of my hair, see, that people and me don't get along. Ever since I was a kid, other folks was bustin' up over my hair. Girls in the schoolyard would call me Curly or Friz or Poodlehead! But I didn't let the name callin' get in my craw. I just took it.

LENNY: You didn't fight 'em?

CURLY: 'Course not. My real name was Thelma. Still, the constant joshin' started eatin' away inside my belly like a canker. 'Fore long I was goin' mad with hate.

LENNY: Was ya mean-mad?

CURLY: No, just first-level mad. But I had no place to pour out my boilin' hate, so I joined 4-H. In the fields I planted clover like a demon, determined to make it grow. The rest of the club did nothing but macrame'n, so I busted some legs and forced 'em into field labor. Sunk all the dues in the treasury into a small fruit stand and worked it into the biggest peach and grape ranch in the tri-county! And still, everybody calls me Curly!

LENNY: Maybe they call ya Curly 'cause of yer your hair.

(CURLY *looks stunned.*)

LENNY: I like your hair. It's looks like it's real soft and manageable.

CURLY: I swear you could cut your fingers on it.

LENNY: I think it looks pertty.

CURLY: Touch it, you'll see.

LENNY: Joad says I can't touch hair no more—

CURLY: *(Forcing* LENNY's *hand on her head)* Touch it!!

LENNY: Yeah, okay.

(LENNY *strokes* CURLY's *hair, cautiously.* CURLY *leans her head onto* LENNY's *shoulder, cautiously.*)

CURLY: How come nobody treats me like a lady, Lenny?

LENNY: I don't know. How come you wear a leather glove with rocks in it?

CURLY: Is that what people say? *(She removes her leather glove to reveal a delicate pearl-covered lace glove beneath.)*

LENNY: *(Delighted)* Ooooo, purty.

CURLY: I got this glove from my mama just before she died.

LENNY: That was nice of her.

CURLY: Not really. She was sinking in quicksand at the time. This glove is all I could get of her. It's the only femi-nine thing I own. Her last words to me were, "Thelma, I'm sorry you got the extra chromasome." I wear this glove in mama's memory. And every morning, I'm reminded of my own femininity, by its reflection in the mirror—as I'm shaving. But I keep it

ACT TWO 55

covered with this leather one. Like a woman in a man's world.

LENNY: I think you'd a made a good lady.

CURLY: Ha. Truth is I never had a date. Never went to a dance, even.

LENNY: I'd like to dance with you, Thelma.

CURLY: Why, Lenny, that's the kindest thing any man has ever said to me.

(CURLY and LENNY come together to dance.)

CURLY: You tell anyone we're doin' this and I'll kick your ass.

LENNY: Okay.

(They dance to slow country tune.)

CURLY: You ever dance before, Lenny?

LENNY: Aunt Clara took me dancin' once but I got sent home early.

CURLY: Why?

LENNY: I killed a mouse.

CURLY: What kinda dance would send you home for that?

LENNY: Disney Costume Cavalcade.

(As CURLY and LENNY dance, they become entangled. Finally, LENNY accidently suffocates CURLY.)

LENNY: *(Noticing that CURLY has passed out)* Oh, Mrs Poodlehead! Oh no, I done bad again.

CROWD OUTSIDE: *(At the square dance)*
Casy, Casy, he's our man
Chunk-a-hurtin'-hard-mean-mad!

LENNY: Oh, no. Oh, no. This is just like Weed, 'cept her head's still on. OH! Hide! Joad said if anything bad happened like in Weed to go hide. But where?

Under the...in the...Rrrr, rrr, Rover's room...rrr...rubber biscuit! Rubber Bed. Bed! That's it! The Ruv... Riv... *(He looks and sees.)* The Reverend's bed! Hide under the Reverend's bed!

CROWD OUTSIDE: *(Approaching door. Chanting)* Un-ion, un-ion, un-ion...

(LENNY hides under the bed just as CANDY, CASY *and* TOM *enter excitedly. They do not see* CURLY *at first.)*

CASY: *(Gesturing to outside)* Listen to it, Tom! That's the noise of union being birthed and we done it! Pickers and drivers and mechanics all makin' demands at the top o' their lungs so's no one can hear a thing. Yer speech you wrote out fer me was poetic, Tom. You done a service.

TOM: But the way you delivered it, Casy, is what got the crowd all riled up. When you put that jap lantern on yer head and stood in the punch bowl and gargled "This Land is Your Land" we all was like to cry. It was inspired, almost like you was sermonizing again.

CASY: I ain't a preacher no more. I'm a mob boss now. Candy, what did we come in here for?

CANDY: We need fliers to send to the other camps, Boss. They's all with us!

TOM: I'll git 'em. *(He moves toward the place where* CURLY *is.)* What the hell?

CASY: What is it, Tom?

TOM: Curly's layin' over here.

CASY: Passed out?

TOM: *(Checks* CURLY*)* Dead. Rib cage been caved in.

CANDY: Those dents in her hair look like paw prints.

CASY: Where's Lenny?

ACT TWO 57

TOM: You don't think that Lenny had anything to do with this, do ya?

CASY: All I know is that the Benevolent Peach Pickers Local just named Curly there an enemy of the worker. If'n the cops find her dead the same night as the rally, they's comin' after us and the union is gonna be outlawed. We can't git the blame, Tom.

CANDY: *(At door, looking out)* Casy, come here and look! The men are burning a scarecrow dressed up like an effigy o' Curly. Even got a poodle tied to the head.

*(*CASY *crosses to door and looks out with* CANDY. LENNY *pokes his head out from under the bed to see.* TOM *notices* LENNY.*)*

TOM: Ah, no!

*(*LENNY *hides again.)*

CANDY: What is it, Tom?

TOM: Nothing. Just thinkin' bout that poodle. *(He takes* CURLY's *gun from her holster and hides it.)* Look here! Just noticed something. Curly's gun is missin'.

CASY: Whoever kill'd her musta took it with 'em.

CANDY: It's Lenny. We all knows it's him. The longer we give him to escape, the more in dutch we'll be by mornin'. He's gotta be brought in to pay for this. With unions, one man ain't all that important. It's all men being cohesified into one that's important. Good pay for an honest day's work. Dental care by someone operatin' out of an office 'stead of a car. Children getting clothed and fed when a man get's laid up or when he—

TOM: I KNOW! I wrote the damn speech! Casy, you and Candy go form a posse. I told Lenny of a secret place to go if'n he ever got in trouble, a cave in a river bed.

LENNY: *(From under bed. Slaps his head.)* Oh!

TOM: *(Thinking)* 'Cept that river was in Oklahoma and even Lenny ain't that dumb. He'd head fer the mountains.

CASY: All right, let's go. You comin', Tom?

TOM: No.

CASY: I understand.

(CANDY *and* CASY *exit.*)

TOM: Lenny, you can come out now. *(Pause)* Lenny?!

LENNY: Jus' a minute, Joad. Be right out.

TOM: I mean it, Lenny. You done somethin' bad and we need to talk about it right now.

(LENNY *climbs out from under the bed with a mouse trap containing a dead mouse.*)

LENNY: Look, Joad, my mouse got himself caught in a trap. Can I save him, Joad? Save him and keep him?

TOM: Sure, Lenny. Why don't you go take a seat over at the table and focus your attention on it.

(LENNY *goes to the table and sits in a chair facing* TOM.)

LENNY: Okay. I'll keep him until we git our rabbits, okay, Joad?

TOM: Okay. Sit the other way, Lenny.

(LENNY *switches to a chair facing away from* TOM, *who prepares to shoot* LENNY *with the gun.*)

LENNY: *(To mouse)* Ow. The trap's squished ya some, but I bet a rub down will make it feel better. There. *(He strokes mouse.)*

(MA *enters in a tizzy.* TOM *hides gun and moves to her, preventing her from seeing* CURLY.)

MA: Tommy, what's the ruckus? Preacher's got himself a gang o' men sayin' theys out trackin' a killer. They got guns, Tommy. You ain't done nothin' rash have ya?

TOM: Naw. Ever'thin's in hand, Ma. I jus' need ya outside fer a while.

LENNY: Hi, Mrs Ma Joad. Got me a mouse, see? Still breathin' too.

MA: *(To* LENNY*)* Nice. *(To* TOM*)* Somethin's wrong, ain't it, Tommy? I know it in your face. What's eatin' ya?

(TOM *shows* CURLY's *body to* MA.)

MA: Land o' Goshen! Is Curly dead, Tommy?

TOM: Kill'd dead.

MA: I know'd it, Tommy. I know'd you couldn't control your hate. Prison's what done it to ya, made ya full o' mean-mad. Hot, grisly mean-mad chuck o' hurtin'—

TOM: Naw, Lenny did it.

MA: *(Disappointed)* Oh.

TOM: Ma, Lenny's got hisself in bad trouble. I can't let 'em lock Lenny up again. I know you don't understand, but I can't.

MA: Tommy, we all know that you and Lenny's got some kinda...special bond. Lord knows we never understood it, but we knows it's there, and we respects it.

TOM: I know if'n Lenny went to prison without someone to look out fer him, he'd go mad fer sure.

(LENNY, *thinking his mouse has stopped breathing, performs C P R on it, pumping its chest with his palms a few times.*)

MA: If'n Lenny went mad...*(Noticing* LENNY*)* how would you know? He's gotta go to jail, Tommy. If'n Lenny runs off, you'd go to jail fer aidin' a felon.

TOM: I ain't goin' to prison, Ma. And Lenny ain't neither. You and Pa never did teach us much stuff like book learnin' or hygiene, but you always teached us to do what we thought was right. I gotta put Lenny at ease before the posse gits him, Ma. I gotta do it.

(TOM *shows gun to* MA. *A touching silent moment of understanding.*)

MA: I understand, Tommy. *(Pause)* Watch the table cloth. *(She exits.)*

LENNY: Okay, roll over so's I can do your stomach. Roll over.

TOM: Lenny, 'member in Oklahoma when we had hat pig and we was fixin' to leave?

LENNY: I remember, Joad. You said it was better if'n we kill'd it fer it's own good 'cause nobody would feed it or water it and it was better to blow it away than let it suffer.

TOM: That's right.

LENNY: Can we have pigs at our place, Joad? If I promise to take care of 'em.

TOM: Sure, Lenny. Why don't you think about the farm we was goin' to git. *(He raises gun and stands behind* LENNY.*)*

LENNY: We'll have a big 'ol place, biggest farm you ever seen. We'll have rabbits in every color: red 'n yellow, black 'n white; and we'll raise alfalfa so's I can cut it and feed it to the rabbits. And we'll work when we want to, and we'll eat what we raise and we'll live off the fatta the land. The fatta the land, Joad.

(BLAM! TOM *fires a shot into the back of* LENNY*'s head. Pause.* LENNY *fidgets slightly, moves his mouth around, then spits the bullet into a nearby bucket.*)

ACT TWO

LENNY: And we'll have chickens and goats, too, and little pups to play with. When we want to eat chicken we'll eat chicken and when we want a goat...

(BLAM! Pause. BLAM! BLAM!)

LENNY: ...we'll have a goat. A billy goat. A silly, willy, little billy...

(LENNY collapses onto the table. After a moment, MA enters.)

MA: You finished, Tommy?

TOM: Yeah, it's done.

MA: *(Taking gun)* You done good. Could maybe use a little target practice, though. Won't be long 'fore the posse comes runnin' back to check out them shots. You'll hav'ta go into hidin' fer a while.

TOM: Yeah, I know.

(CASY enters.)

CASY: Tom? Tom? Is you all right?

TOM: Fine enough fer a wanted man, I guess.

CASY: *(Noticing LENNY)* Holy moley mother o' God. Someone shot Lenny!

MA: *(Still holding gun)* Tommy done it.

CASY: Dammit, Tom. I know you wouldn't do somethin' less you thought it were fer the best. No matter how careless and stupid it might appear from the outside. But we can't harbor ya, Tom. Not after this.

TOM: I know. I don't expect ya to. I was thinkin' about somethin' you said once, Casy, 'bout a guy not havin' a soul but bein' part of a bigger one. People out there needs to know that, needs someone to show 'em. Maybe that's where I'll hide fer a while. Out there, among the people.

MA: But where will you be, Tommy?

TOM: *(Subtle music)* I'll be everywhere—everywhere ya look. Wherever they's a fight so hungry folks can eat, I'll be there...

(Suddenly, LENNY lets out a moan and tries to get up from the table. Music stops.)

LENNY: Oooohhhh.

TOM: What the hell?

MA: Lenny ain't dead? Thought fer sure he was dead!

CASY: Uh, come on over here to the bed, Lenny.

(CASY and TOM lead LENNY to the bed.)

CASY: You'll be right as rain. *(To TOM)* Tom, your Ma and I'll hold him down; you go git the shovel.

(CASY sits and LENNY lays with his head on CASY's lap.)

MA: *(Kneels and comforts LENNY)* Ain't no need fer that. The boy's dyin', you can see it in his eyes. You rest for now, Lenny.

LENNY: *(Weakly)* I'm hungry, Joad.

CASY: *(To TOM)* Says he's hungry. Got somethin'? Anythin' fer his dyin' sperit?

TOM: I don't know. Ma?

MA: Not a thing, Tommy. Them peaches cleaned us out. The cupboard's nothin' but cobwebs and we ain't got the money to afford the store.

LENNY: Miiiiiiiiilk. I want a glass o' milk, Joad.

CASY: Says he wants milk.

MA: Don't know how.

CASY: Unless... *(An idea!)* Ma, I know this may be difficult, but if'n you could undo your dress and pull out yer breast. We could raise poor Lenny's mouth to

ACT TWO 63

your nip, and even if yer dry, you'd comfort his mortal hour with the milk of the human kindness.

LENNY: Miiiiiilk.

MA: I suddenly remember a pint of half'n'half I left in the truck. I'll go fetch it!

LENNY: Aghh! *(He collapses to the floor, dead. We assume it's for good.)*

CASY: Don't bother, Mrs Joad. Lenny's gone. *(Removes his hat and turns to* TOM*)* I'm sorry, Tom, but I knows he's better off now.

TOM: I don't know if'n there's a paradise, Casy, the kind you used to tell of with a Garden of Eden and all. But if there is, Lenny's in it. And the rabbits is pissed.

CANDY: *(Distant voice)* This way! You men, come with me!

MA: Tommy, they's comin'! You gotta git outta here til things cool off.

TOM: I know. I'll take the gun, Ma, and I'm takin' the blame too. Stick with Casy or go back to Oklahoma, I'll find ya.

MA: Don't worry none about me, I got the union. What about you, Tommy? Where was it you said you was goin'?

(Music up)

TOM: I'll be ever'where—everywhere you look. Wherever there's a fight so hungry folks can eat, I'll be there. Wherever there's a cop beatin' up a guy, I'll be there. I'll be hidin' in the bushes, but I'll be there. Wherever there's a girl on a street corner handin' out free packs of cigarettes, I'll be there too. I'll be there in the way farm folks laugh 'cause they's gettin' subsidy checks just to take their land outta production; or in the way kids yell 'cause they's eatin' fer free in a school lunch program and it's pizza day! That's where you'll find me, Ma. All around. Everywhere.

MA: I don't understand, Tommy.

TOM: It's jus' some stuff I been thinkin' about. *(Turning to* CASY*)* Bye, Jim Casy.

CASY: The union'll name an expressway after ya, Tom.

TOM: Goodbye, Ma.

MA: Goodbye, Tommy. *(Gives* TOM *the Happy Rub)*

*(*TOM *checks to see if it's safe, turns and looks back, then exits.* CASY *crosses, surveys the scene, and slowly turns to* MA*.)*

MA: I give him a week.

(Lights drop to black.)

END OF PLAY

PROPERTY LIST

Crates and household goods for opening scene
Bulldozer brake lever
"Condemned by Owner" forms
Mouse
Matchbook
Knapsack
Flask
Handbill
Shovel
Briefcase with papers
Shotgun or rifle
Old photograph
Baby shoes
Huge foam-rubber cowboy hat
Prison souvenir T-shirt
Dustball
Doughnuts
Coffee pot, coffee cup
Catsup & sugar dispensers
Radio
Truck radiator
Wrapped loaf of bread
Candy jars with penny candy
Pine auto air freshener display
Clothespins altered to fit over noses
Clipboard
Grape crate with D D T label and grapes

Buckets
Lantern
Small bag of peaches
Handgun & holster
Whip
Receipt
CURLY coin *(fake money)*
Bag with union flyers
Stew pot, bowls & spoons
Red bandanas
Mousetrap

www.ingramcontent.com/pod-product-compliance
Lightning Source LLC
Chambersburg PA
CBHW060216050426
42446CB00013B/3090